YOUR KNOWLEDGE HAS VALUE

Imprint:

Copyright © 2017 GRIN Verlag, Open Publishing GmbH
Print and binding: Books on Demand GmbH, Norderstedt Germany
ISBN: 9783668587359

This book at GRIN:

http://www.grin.com/en/e-book/383163/quantified-personality-automatic-persona-lity-analysis-from-online-and

Steffen Schumacher

Quantified Personality. Automatic Personality Analysis from Online and Mobile Usage Data

GRIN Publishing

GRIN - Your knowledge has value

Since its foundation in 1998, GRIN has specialized in publishing academic texts by students, college teachers and other academics as e-book and printed book. The website www.grin.com is an ideal platform for presenting term papers, final papers, scientific essays, dissertations and specialist books.

Visit us on the internet:

http://www.grin.com/

http://www.facebook.com/grincom

http://www.twitter.com/grin_com

Quantified Personality – Automatic Personality Analysis from Online and Mobile Usage Data

Steffen Schumacher
11/2017

Algorithms are instructions for the stepwise execution of a method. Social and cultural scientists but tend to broaden the meaning of this notion and use it as an umbrella notion for digital automatization in general. But computer programs contain non-algorithmic command syntax, also. Furthermore, algorithms may develop and change during implementation and use which makes talking about "the" algorithm being always identical with itself often difficult or impossible. A comprehension of the notion of algorithm too distant from that of computer science hinders the comprehensibility of social and cultural scientific analyses by computer scientists. On the other hand, these sciences shouldn't confine their usage of this notion to that of the latter to be still able to deal with the phenomenon from a different perspective. (cf. Dourish 2016)

Automatic personality analysis doesn't use data gathered by questionnaires administered to respondents, any more, but uses usage data which are generated by default and in different contexts, respectively. This is the big novelty of this field of investigation which led to the two articles published by Kosinski and Stillwell in the „Proceedings of the National Academy of Sciences of the United States of America" in 2013 and 2015 being the most influential articles ever published in the "Proceedings" according to their Altmetric Score. These two articles dealt with the analysis of the personality of Facebook users using their Facebook likes.

Since automated personality analysis is based on Big Data - for the development of its methods as well as their application - it is subject to the three paradoxes of Big Data described by Richards and King (2013): 1. The transparency paradox which follows from collecting more and more data to be able to make the world more transparent, but collecting them in more and more invisible and opaque ways. The data are saved on servers in unknown places and are analysed by methods and algorithms which are not easy to scrutinize. This holds in general, i.e. also for data and methods of automatic personality analysis.

2. The identity paradox: voluminous online usage data are analysed to reveal the behaviour and preferences – and in the future also the personality – of users, but the results are applied to influence and modify these very behaviours and preferences. Like in the case of filter bubbles generated by automated news feeds which send users only those informations which already conform to their preferences. The aim of automated personality analysis, too, is to be able to choose content and layout of advertising and political messages this way that they appeal to the users' personality. Also, commercial websites and services and the behaviour of virtual agents should be able to be tailored to the individual users alike. Is there a personality bubble afoot which exceeds the filter bubble and renders the digital environment of the users accomodated to their personality to the maximum?

3. The third Big Data paradox which is linked to the first two is the power paradox which consists in the fact that, on the one hand side, Big Data should help everybody to gain informations about the world and to communicate with other users, but, on the other hand side, the very usage traces of the users doing this are stored and can be used by big organizations as well as agencies which have the right to access them to gain informations about the users and control them. This risk is particularly high in the case of automated personality analysis, since it yields intimate knowledge about the individuals' personality and, thus, can uncover their weak points and ways to influence them.

Automatic personality analysis is a very recent field of investigation. The first summary article of it was published in 2014 (Vinciarelli 2014). According to it, the number of articles which have the notion "personality" in their title and have been published in journals of the two biggest international organizations of computer science and computer scientists, ACM and IEEE [1], jumped up in 2010. All articles found by me and dealt with in the following sections have been published in 2011 and afterwards, almost all of them in journals of the two professional organizations. By far most of the authors have a degree in computer science, followed by psychology and psychometrics.

In all articles, the model of personality used is the Big Five personality model, a psychological personality model which assumes the personality of every human being consisting of five dimensions which can be developed stronger or weaker. These five dimensions are called personality traits. They are openness, conscientiousness, extraversion, agreeableness and neuroticism. [2] That it is a psychological personality model means that values and attitudes which belong to the personality of individuals, too, aren't investigated. [3] The Big Five model is the most widespread and accepted one in current psychology and possesses significant relations to external variables like job satisfaction, occupational position and achievement as well as choice of spouse and friends (Golbeck et al. 2011a).

In a study of employees of the IBM Almaden Research Center (Gou et al. 2014), two further models of personality have been used for analysis: the „basic human values" of Shalom H. Schwartz – self-transcendence, conservation, self-enhancement, openness to change and hedonism – as well as a model which is developed by the authors themselves and based on Maslow's hierarchy of needs and on marketing literature. It is called „fundamental needs" and includes ideals, harmony, closeness, self-expression, excitement and curiosity.

It has to be said that the Big Five model has been critized in particular in regard to its intra-individual stability over time (Neuman 2016: 13), i.e. in regard to its test-retest-reliability.

The first kind of data which has been used to extract the personality of users are smartphone usage data or mobile phone usage data in general (mobile usage data).

There are a number of articles which describe studies with mobile phone users. The latter fill in a personality questionnaire, and either their smartphone usage data are recorded by an app – call logs, SMS logs, app logs, Bluetooth scans of the environment and profile logs, i.e. logs of the adjustments of their smartphone profile, as well as heart rate, GPS position and derived walking speed, speed-up, duration of sleep, light intensity, pressure [4] - or mobile usage data are used which are stored by their mobile provider, i.e. metadata. Between personality and usage data, a mathematical connection is searched for by methods like regression and correlational analysis. This is the general procedure for the development of algorithms and programs for personality analysis: they are always based on formulae generated by connecting personality data from questionnaires to other kind of data which are later used to extract the personality of their authoring users whithout them having filled in a personality questionnaire.

In a study from 2011 (Chittaranjan et al. 2011), a large number of usage log data serve as independent variables which have been stored from 83 test persons during a period of eight

---

[1] The Association for Computing Machinery (ACM) is the biggest international organization of computer science and the Institute for Electrical and Electronics Engineers (IEEE) is the biggest international professional organization of engineers from the area of electrical engineering and communications technology.

[2] The model is often called OCEAN model according to the acronym built from the notions for the five dimensions in this order.

[3] But they are investigated by the techniques of sentiment analysis and opinion mining aiming at individuals' positive and negative attitudes to objects (Liu/Zhang 2013). These attitudes can be rather short-time and ephemeral, e.g. concerning products and services, which one wouldn't conceive of as part of the individuals' personality.

[4] Imaginable would be also die usage of data which could be transmitted to the smartphone by wearable devices like smart watches and fitness wristbands.

months by a specialised software: use of the Office software, internet, video, audio, maps, Youtube, calendar functions, camera, chat functionality, SMS and games, number of outgoing calls, duration of outgoing calls (in average and in total), number of incoming calls, duration of incoming calls (in average and in total), number of emails sent and received, number of SMS sent and received, word length in emails sent and received (in average and the median value), number of contacts, number of telephone numbers called and having called, the same for SMS contacts etc. Big Five traits were used. A regression analysis with all these variables as independent variables reached an increase in accuracy of personality prediction of 17 to 40 percent for the five personality traits compared with prediction by chance (25 percent in average, extraversion and neuroticism were predicted best). This means a correct classification of the Big Five personality of 69 to 76 percent of the individuals. The interpretation of the relations found isn't easy, partly they are directly plausibel, partly not. E.g. it's plausibel that extraverted persons got more calls and these calls lasted longer. But there didn't exist the same relation for outgoing calls. Another example: the authors explain their finding that one and the same Bluetooth ids were found more often in the environment of more emotionally stable (i.e. less neurotic) as well as more agreeable persons by speculating about persons possessing these personality traits staying a longer time in one and the same place than other persons.

In two studies from 2011 and 2013 (Oliveira et al. 2011, Montjoye et al. 2013), the data used are exclusively from call detail records (CDR) of mobile providers, i.e. from metadata of calls, SMS and MMS of mobile phone users. These are e.g. the number of calls, SMS and MMS, outgoing as well as incoming, the duration of calls, the interval between receipt of text messages and reply to them and between telephone calls with one and the same contact (phone number) and the ratio between the number of calls and text messages and the number of contacts. So, it's not necessary to record the smartphone usage behaviour as described above, any more. These two studies used the Big Five model, too. The mean increase in accuracy of prediction of the Big Five traits against prediction by chance is higher than in the study described above: 39 percent (of variance) and 42 percent (concerning the classification of individuals into the three categories low, middle, high per trait), respectively. While in Oliveira et al. 2011 extraversion and neuroticism could be predicted best, like in Chittaranjan et al. 2011, it were openness and conscientiousness in the study of Montjoye et al. from 2013. After the additional inclusion of properties of the personal network of the individuals like number of contacts, network density and number of frequent contacts, openness was predicted best in the former study and neuroticism worst which pattern can be often found in studies described below using data from social networks.

I haven't found studies using smartphone usage data after the year 2013. In an article from 2016 (Guo 2016), considerations are at least made about which smartphone usage data could be appropriate for the analysis of the users' personality, but they aren't tested empirically: physical data like heart rate and GPS position as well as users' preferences being identified through their browsing histories.

The second kind of data used in studies of automatic personality analysis are Facebook likes. These data have been successfully used and made famous by Michael Kosinski, a psychologist and psychological programmer, and David Stillwell, a psychologist and psychometrician, as already mentioned above. One reason for their success was their way of formulating the degrees of accuracy of prediction reached: they equated them with the accuracy of judgement of acquaintances, friends and spouses. Both authors were employed at the centre of psychometrics of the University of Cambridge in 2013. In 2015, Kosinski had changed to Stanford University. They used the Big Five personality model, too.

In the first of their two pertinent articles (Kosinski et al. 2013), they predict not only the Big Five traits of individuals, but also personal properties like sexual orientation, sex, age, race and political affiliation from Facebook likes, the second article deals only with the Big Five traits (Youyou et al. 2015). In both articles, they use data from tens of thousands of people which have filled in a Big Five personality questionnaire in a Facebook app called myPersonality (which had been developed by Stillwell) and, at the same time, have agreed to the usage of their personality as well as Facebook profile data for scientific purposes. In total, 7.5 million Facebook user have filled in at least one of the personality questionnaires from the app which included 20 to 100 questions (Schwartz et al. 2013: 6) during the period between 2007 and 2012 when the app was online. Other psychometric tests could be made in it, too. Their data are used in the article from 2015 for external validation of the personality measures. To motivate participants to make tests from the app they could view their results afterwards. Facebook likes had been publicly accessible by API from 2009 to April 30th 2015 (Anonymous 2016), so, they respresented a publicly available stock of data during these years. In their article from 2015, the authors work with data of 70.000 users which all had filled in the 100 item Big Five questionnaire. More than 17.000 of them had been rated by a Facebook friend in regard to their personality by means of a 10 item Big Five questionnaire. And 14.000 of them had been rated by a second Facebook friend, so that the agreement between both judgements could be measured, in these cases. By means of a regression analysis, the relation between Facebook likes and Big Five traits were computed and, after this, it was tested how good the personality traits of those participants could be predicted which hadn't been used to compute the formula, but had been spared for testing. These were a tenth of the sample. The accuracy of the prediction of a person's personality increased plausibly with the number of Facebook likes included. The authors obtained thresholds of accuracy of prediction from a meta-analysis of published study results, namely the accuracy of colleagues, cohabitants, friends and partners in assessing one's personality by a questionnaire. This accuracy was expressed in Pearson's correlation coefficients. The result of their regression analysis was that with ten Facebook likes included in the analysis one's personality – cast as the mean of the Big Five traits – could be assessed better than by a colleague, with 70 Facebook likes better than by a friend or cohabitant, with 150 likes better than by a family member and with 300 likes better than by a spouse. [5] Furthermore, the congruence between judgements of different judges were higher in the case of algorithms than of human beings. In the former case, different judges were two independently computed algorithms each based on one randomly chosen half of the likes used. Finally, personality assessment by algorithms also correlated better with human behaviour and other aspects having been extracted from the participants' Facebook profiles and from the other psychometric tests of the app: study subject, size of the personal network on Facebook, substance use, health, activities on Facebook, attitudes like party preference, general values and life satisfaction as well as depression. The authors conclude that Facebook likes were a better predictor of human personality than the social cognitive abilities of human beings. The latter would be influenced by factors external to the task in question. Computers could, thus, assess humans' personality better than other humans. On the other hand side, the authors give in that personality was limited to the Big Five traits, here, and that there could possibly be other, e.g. more subtle, personality traits which weren't measured by the Big Five questionnaire and could be only recognized by fellow human beings, so far.

So, they could formulate the results of their study of Facebook likes in a very handy way: to assess someone better than a friend or cohabitant when useing 70 likes, better than a family member when using 150 likes and even better than a spouse when using 300 likes. Naturally, this shows the data drivenness of their approach which is adopted by many Big Data projects: research doesn't follow from a theory nor aims at it, but investigates a stock of data on the

---

[5] Openness was the Big Five trait which could be predicted best. From the other four traits which were close together in this respect neuroticism was predicted worst.

basis of rather basic assumptions or simply because of their availability. This research doesn't in practice deal so much with users' personality, but with attributes like creditworthiness, purchasing power, likelihood of the cancellation of credits and health forecast (Christl 2014).

For the practical purpose of data driven research, it suffices if the formula found works. There isn't a need for explanation why it works. In my opinion, this implies that it can't be predicted if the independent variables' power of prediction changes over time, e.g. decreases, if their value or their overall quality largely change. This means that the formulae used for prediction must be monitored and updated regularly since it can't be known with sincerity that the relations found still exist and haven't changed, respectively.

One general assumption about the reason for the ability of Facebook likes to predict users' personality is made by Youyou, Kosinski and Stillwell (2015):

"Why are Likes diagnostic of personality? Exploring the Likes most predictive of a given trait shows that they represent activities, attitudes, and preferences highly aligned with the Big Five theory. For example, participants with high openness to experience tend to like Salvador Dalí, meditation, or TED talks; participants with high extraversion tend to like partying, Snookie (reality show star), or dancing." (Youyou et al. 2015: 2)

It's plausible that likes have something to do with users' attitudes, preferences and activities, because they are the result of an evaluation by them. Though, a theory proper is missing, here. And they don't build one from the results of their study, also.

I remains to be said that their results relate to the mean value of the five personality traits as already mentioned above. This traits are but predicted with differing accuracy: openness best, conscientiousness and neuroticism worst. Reasons for these differences aren't given by the authors. So, they stick to this very unspecific explanation.

An additional question is if their method is still useful today since Facebook likes aren't freely accessible any more.

Digression: The role of automatic personality analysis based on Facebook likes in the US election campaigns from 2016

After Trump's election victory, the US enterprise Cambridge Analytica claimed to have made this victory possible by the psychographic analysis of the electorate which had taken place also on the basis of Facebook likes. By this, Trump's campaign staff had been enabled to address voters in a more effective way (Confessore et al. 2017). This enterprise seems to have recruited some employees from the University of Cambridge and also chosen his name in connection with it. Of course, such a name also carries the good reputation of this institution. According to press reports, Michael Kosinski blames the enterprise to have stolen the method of personality analysis from Facebook likes, facilitated perhaps by the contact to members of the Centre for Psychometrics of the University for which he and Stillwell worked and work, respectively (Grassegger et al. 2016, Hartlmaier et al. 2017: 35f.). Meanwhile, Cambridge Analytica had to abandon his grandiose claims. It had worked only on a part of Trump's campaign and had done only conventional statistical, not psychographic, voter analysis in it (Beuth 2017). But it's a matter of fact that it is making an effort to buy as much data allowing a psychographic analysis about as many US citizens as possible. E.g. to get the permission for the usage of Facebook likes which weren't publicly accessible at the time of the US election campaign, any more, it used a quiz game app and some other smaller Big Five test apps which request access to the individuals' Facebook likes if they want to do the quiz and tests (Grassegger et al. 2016).

Cambridge Analytica is partly owned by a rich supporter of the US Conservative Party, Robert Mercer, had firstly worked for the presidential campaign of the Conservative Ted Cruz, then, after Cruz withdrew, for that of Trump (Lapowsky 2016). Robert Mercer incidentally finances also Breitbart News, the infamous right-wing news portal for which Steve Bannon worked and, after leaving the White House, works again. Bannon had a seat in the board of management of Cambridge Analytica for some time. Thus far the connections between an enterprise doing psychographic analysis and the political realm even though psychography/ psychometry wasn't applied in the 2016 US presidential campaign as explicated above. But through the wrong claims of the enterprise, the psychographic method of voter analysis gained the attention of the media and the public. (Grassegger et al. 2016, Confessore et al. 2017)

To lead over to the third data category – text data -, I deal with a study from 2011 which analyses the personality of Facebook users using their Facebook profiles (Golbeck et al. 2011b). The number of test persons is 167 and, thus, quite small, again. The personality model used is the Big Five model whose data were collected from the test persons by means of a questionnaire. The study found that profile features like number of friends, density of the friends network, i.e. the share of friends who knew other friends of the same user, relationship status, length of surname, length of the activity list and of the list of favourite books correlated significantly with at least one of the Big Five traits. But most features which were extracted from the Facebook profiles were word counts from the status updates as well as the about-me and the blurb texts. At this point, it is already text data which were used. The authors of the study analysed these text parts of the profiles with a famous, often used computer program, the Linguistic Inquiry and Word Count (LIWC), which counts the words of which texts consist and assign them to 81 different categories which fall into five upper categories: psychological processes (emotional, cognitive, sensoric, social), relativity (relating to time, the past and the future), personal aspects (like job, financial themes, health) and a miscellaneous category (like punctuation marks, swearwords). The authors could predict the Big Five traits through regression on these independent variables with a mean absolute error of 11 percent which seems to be a quite good accuracy. They used cross validation, i.e. they computed a number of regression models each time excluding another portion of the test persons from the computation to use them to test the model, afterwards.

It's also interesting that Kosinski and Stillwell investigated Twitter profile data as basis for personality analysis prior to their Facebook likes based method (Quercia et al. 2011): the number of Twitter users followed by the profile owner himself, the number of the profile owners' own followers and the frequency of the profile owners' appearance on reading lists of other Twitter users, i.e. they didn't use text data. Two measures of the influence which Twitter users have within the internet were also included, one of them employs also the number of the users' Facebook contacts. All these profile data are publicly accessible. 335 persons were investigated which had done the Big Five personality test on Stillwells myPersonality app und had disclosed the link to their Twitter account. The authors used a regression analysis with tenfold cross validation. The square root of the mean square deviation of the predicted from the real values (mean of the five traits) was 0.88 on a scale of one to five which is a very good accuracy according to the authors.

I got the impression that this path – the analysis of social media profiles – hasn't been followed any longer after the year 2011, and the focus has been put on Facebook likes and text data. Nonetheless, there are some interesing and plausible correlations with Big Five traits in these studies. The number of Facebook friends correlates significantly positively with the trait extraversion, but network density negatively just as with openness. The explanation given by the authors is that extraverted and open individuals had many and varied Facebook friends which knew each other more seldomly than those of persons with other personality traits because of their heterogeneity. The number of persons which one follows on Twitter as well as the number of own Twitter followers are correlated positively with extraversion and negatively with neuroticism which is plausibly explained by Quercia et al. with extraverts' constantly high readiness to communicate and the opposite attitude of neurotic persons. No explanation is given for the significantly positive correlation of standing on the reading list of other Twitter users with openness, but not with extraversion, too. They only hint at openness being linked to individual attributes like imaginative, spontaneous and adventurous. So, perhaps, tweets of open persons are written in a particularly interesting way and contain more often new informations.

Let's turn to the third data category, text data which can be published on various online sites, e.g. in social media (Twitter, Facebook, Instagram) and in forums and blogs. The procedure of analysis is similar to that using smartphone data and Facebook likes: regression models or machine learning algorithms (e.g. decision trees) [6] are developed from texts of whose authors the personality traits are known (collected from a questionnaire) and, then, can be applied to texts of users whose personality is not known to analyse it within the Big Five framework. [7] Measures extracted from the texts are most often word frequencies (so-called word count approach (Schwartz et al. 2013: 2)), sometimes also the frequency of phrases (combinations of words) and themes (clusters of words). A further discriminating feature between methods of this kind is if the words to be counted are taken from already existing, psychologically annotated lexicons - collections of words -, e.g. the LIWC (see above), hoping that the psychological categories included are somehow linked to the personality dimensions or traits in a statistically feasible way. Or if these words are based on the kind of texts to be analysed themselves and, thus, no preselection is made on the basis of existing word categorizations. Schwartz et al. (2013) call this the closed vs. the open vocabulary approach.

Neuman (2016, chap. 4) describes in his book a method he developed which utilizes word frequencies, the so-called vectorial semantics approach of personality analysis. It compares the frequency of selected words from the text data with their frequency in a corpus of texts stemming from authors with known Big Five personality traits. For this purpose, he identifies a set of words to be counted for each trait since being related to it in the text corpus, i.e. being frequently used in it by owners of the respective trait (closed vocabulary approach). Concretely, he marks the word frequencies on coordinate axes and draws the vector from the coordinate origin to the point which is defined by the coordinates. The angle between the word vector of the text data to be analysed and that of a personality trait in the text corpus yields the degree of proximity of the personality of the text's author to this trait. If the angle is zero proximity is maximal, if it is 90 degrees proximity is minimal.

Neuman built one word vector for each of the Big Five traits from his text corpus and, using them for personality analysis, reached the accuracy of the then current state-of-the-art method. The latter worked with two lexicons, one for the degree of specificity of words and one which contained 585 categories of emotions (expressed by words).

In 2011, a study of the prediction of the personality of Twitter users from their tweets was published (Golbeck et al. 2011a). It was from the same authors who had conducted the above mentioned study using Facebook profiles (Golbeck et al. 2011b). According to the authors, this study was the first to use social media texts for personality analysis. It follows the usual scheme: Big Five traits were collected from the 50 test persons by questionnaire and also the data to be analysed, in this case their up to 2.000 last tweets. They assembled the tweets of each user into a single document for analysis, but also used a few data from the genuine level

---

[6] Machine learning algorithms (ML algorithms) are most often applied to predict the categories of a dichotomous variable (yes, no). Though terms used to denote the relevance of independent variables in this case are different from those of regression models (information content vs. significance), the respective measures can be traced back to statistical significance, too.

[7] So, also in the case of text data, the goal is to yield the structure of users' personality, not their opinions and attitudes. The extraction of the latter from text data is dealt with by methods like opinion mining and sentiment analysis (cf. Liu et al. 2013). These methods face problems like correct understanding of sentences formulated in a neutral, non-judgemental way which nonetheless are meant to express evaluations as well as of irony.

of tweets: the mean number of hashtags, words and web links per tweet. From the document built, they used the number of punctuation marks (comma, period, question mark, exclamation mark and parenthesis) and also the counts of a whole number of word categories taken from two standard lexicons for text analysis, the LIWC and the MRC Psycholinguistic Database. The latter contains linguistic and psycholinguistic properties of 150.000 words, e.g. measures of their familiarity, meaningfulness, concreteness and age of aquisition. They used all these word and feature counts as independent variables of a regression analysis with the Big Five traits as dependent variable. Interestingly, they could predict openness best and neuroticism worst like the method using Facebook likes. The deviation of the predicted from the real values added up to 11 to 18 percent (mean absolute error) for the five separate traits, i.e. it was quite good (small), but higher than in the study using Facebook profile data in which it was 11 percent for all five traits. They but don't mention the statistic significance of their correlations, presumably due to the very small sample that they use. They denominate the relationships found – regression coefficients – partly as intuitively comprehensible, e.g. the negative relation of conscientiousness with negative emotions and its positive one with the use of the pronoun "you" (such people talking more about or to others). Partly, they find them incomprehensible, e.g. the positive relation of agreeableness and openness with the number of parentheses. From that, one can see the data driven approach, again, which uses certain presuppositions – word usage has a relation to personality -, but no elaborated theory, either from the outset or as a result of the investigation (accordingly, just the "intuitive" comprehensibility of the results is considered by the authors). The main goal is to find relations for a satisfactory prediction of the dependent variable. The practical aim is the main aim. Schwartz et al. (2013: 3) speak of prediction vs. insights.

Gou et al. (2014), employed with the IBM Almaden Research Center in San José, USA, used 256 colleagues as test persons and investigated their personality by means of three different questionnaires operationalizing three different models of personality and the possibility to predict it from their 200 latest Twitter tweets. As already mentioned above, the three models are the Big Five model, the "basic human values" of Shalom H. Schwartz and the "fundamental needs model" being developed by the authors themselves. The approach was a closed vocabulary approach, in case of the first two models the LIWC was used for the analysis of tweets, in case of the third model a lexicon developed with assistance of crowd workers. Only the third model had nearly significant relationships, at least, with the word counts which is explained by the authors by the small sample. [8] The correlations between predicted and real personality dimensions found are only small. A linear regression model was used for prediction (Yang et al. 2013). Since no mean absolute error is reported, the

---

[8] In this study and all the more in the studies described above which analyse even smaller samples, though perhaps less biased ones (IBM employees should distinctively be not representative for the population, e.g. in regard to income and school and occupational education), the proclivity of psychologists to analyse just quite small samples can be seen. This is an expression of the outlook that an intact brain always functions the same way, i.e. a natural scientific outlook on the psychic processes involved. But a questionnaire doesn't consist of stimuli in the natural scientific meaning of the word, but of semantic units. The meanings which human beings extract from the latter, and from texts in general, are influenced by their values and world views. These, in turn, depend on their socialisation, group affiliations and individual circumstances, i.e. they vary. Trying to compute generally valid relationships on the basis of such small, non-representative samples is, thus, principally dubious. Even if practical applicability is the goal of the investigation, not the testing or generation of empirical or theoretical propositions, statistical significance should exist. Since the factors of influence mentioned can't be operationalized by variables like gender, age, education, income, nation, culture in the case of automatic personality analysis, just because they are not known of the persons to be analysed, the sample used should be varied enough in regard to these variables, at least, to yield generalizable formulae. So as it can be assumed to be in the case of the very big sample of Kosinski's and Stillwell's analysis of Facebook likes. In the case of psychological studies with small samples, generalizations are feasible at best through a meta-analysis of many of them possessing a broad scope of people investigated, in total. (That's the well-known critique of psychologism and its undersocialized outlook.)

results can't be compared with those of Golbeck et al. (2011a) whose sample was even much smaller.

Interestingly, Gou et al. asked the test persons how satisfied they were with their predicted personality traits. The mean satisfaction was just above a value of three on a scale of one to five for all three personality models. Furthermore, they asked under which conditions they would agree to the disclosure of their personality test results, against which persons and which risks and benefits they expected from it. Though the participants believed informations about their personality to be very personal informations and the risk to exist to be exposed to prejudices, afterwards, almost half of them mentioned benefits like a better mutual understanding, better communication and cooperation, better motivation and rewarding of others. In addition, method and personality traits included should be explained exactly as well as possible flaws to preclude false interpretations. Amount and kind of information disclosed and of data used for personality analysis and the persons against which personal informations would be disclosed should be determined by the persons analysed themselves. They should also be allowed to comment on the results of the analysis and to correct them. The authors of the study ask explicitly how to deal with different results of personality analysis for one and the same person caused by usage of different data sources (e.g. Twitter vs. Facebook text data) and propose a collaboration between analysis system and analysed person to eliminate contradictions.

Schwartz et al. (2013) use Facebook status updates for personality analysis. Kosinski and Stillwell belong to the group of authors, too, so, the up to 75.000 test persons used are from the pool of users of the myPersonality app. The test persons had to be native English speakers, authors of Facebook status updates of at least 1000 words, under 65, with age and gender mentioned in their profile and to have conducted one of the 20 to 100 item Big Five personality tests of the app. They made one analysis with an open vocabulary approach and a second with the closed vocabulary of the LIWC. The result was that the open vocabulary approach could predict the personality of the test persons somewhat better than the LIWC. The square root of the coefficent of determination which expresses the correlation between the predicted and the real Big Five personality traits has values between 0.3 and about 0.4 which are, according to the authors, similar to the maximum correlations between personality dimensions and behaviour. Again, openness to change could be predicted best and neurotisicm worst (together with conscientiousness).

The fourth, only recently used, kind of data are pictures from Instagram, the third of the big social media networks alongside Facebook and Twitter. A study from 2016 (Ferwerda et al. 2016) investigates the statistical relationship between the colour of the pictures and the personality of their owners. Users of Instagram can put filters on the pictures which they have uploaded and change their colour by them. Thus, the colour of the pictures can be manipulated by their owners. For the personality analysis, colour according to the HSV colour model was used since it was most similar to the human visual system. H stands für hue, S for saturation – which is the share of colour vs. the share of whiteness - and V for brightness ("value"). Additionally, the PAD categories (pleasure, arousal, dominance) defined by the values of V and S were used and, finally, the number of human faces and full human figures. From all of these attributes of pictures, the mean value was calculated across all pictures of a user and then fed into the analysis. In total, more than 22.000 pictures of 113 test persons were included. The test persons had filled in a Big Five personality questionnaire. From the correlations of the mean colour and content related attributes, partly directly comprehensible relationships could be derived, partly not. Results were e.g.: open persons have pictures possessing average more green and cold colours, being darker and more saturated und with less human faces and figures. Agreeable persons possess pictures which are less dark and, at the same time, less bright (i.e. have less extreme brightness). Neurotic persons have brighter pictures. Only part of these results make directly sense. The most comprehensible are the relationships to the PAD categories: pictures of open persons express less pleasure, but more arousal and dominance, those of extraverted persons less pleasure, but more dominance, those of neurotic persons more pleasure and less dominance. The main method used for analysis was a regression analysis. Three different kinds of regression analysis, all with tenfold cross validation, were used. Like in many of the studies mentioned above using Facebook likes or text data, openness could be predicted best and neuroticism worst. The square root of the mean square deviation of the predicted from the real values is smaller or only slightly higher for the five personality traits than in the study of Quercia et al. (2011), i.e. has good values for all traits, too.

According to the authors, their study is the first which uses Instagram pictures for personality analysis. It differs from the studies mentioned heretofore in that the authors recur to an already existing theoretical and empirical approach for the justification of the appropriateness of the data for their aim (see p.853).

In summary, it can be said that there exist promising approaches to automatic personality analysis. They use online and mobile usage data collected for other purposes. Only in case of smartphone activity logs, the data used had been collected especially for the purpose of personality analysis, by means of a special software. Because of the small or very small samples of test persons used, except for in the studies using Facebook likes and status updates, methods developed can't but be taken for technically mature. Relations found are rarely significant, again except for in the studies using Facebook likes and status updates. Though, improvement in prediction by the formulae computed and algorithms found is recognizable, but since different measures were used for quality of prediction, not all of the studies can be compared with each other in this respect. Partly, categorizations of the continuous Big Five dimensions are used (low, middle, high), partly, the original values. An accuracy of categorization of between 66 and 75 percent means presumably a good increase in effectivity for the goals of commercial advertisement and electoral propaganda (the base line is not always 50 percent, but can also be higher). But is it high enough for the adaptation of websites, services and, as the most powerful application, virtual agents and robots to the personality of their users? I think this to be the case only if contact to the users isn't too frequent and intense. E.g. with household robots or an often used virtual agent, it shouldn't suffice in practice to classify only two of three or three of four persons rightly. On the other hand side, it's more difficult to determine how to interpret an average error of 10 to 20 percent. It depends on how a conrete application is designed based on these values.

Since none of the online usage data used in the studies (Facebook likes, Twitter tweets, Facebook status updates, pictures from Instagram) are freely accessible any more, today, but only after explicit approval by the users affected, the question about the usefulness of these methods in practice arises. The only feasible way to gain large quantities of user permissions for data access is to get them from users of Facebook or other apps which request them as a precondition of their use. This was the case with Stillwell's myPersonality app which got a very high response. But it seems to be difficult or impossible to get data for personality analysis of a big enough share of the population of a country and, accordingly, of the world population using this way of registration as a user of an app. Thus, the approaches presented show the feasibility of automated personality analysis in principle, only. If users want to profit from automatic personality analysis they have to give explicitly access to their data. Perhaps, in the future, appropriate data will be found which can be freely used (within the legal confines for this method as is already the case for testing for creditworthiness).

After the review of the existing approaches, I'll deal with the purposes of automatic personality analysis mentioned in the studies presented above and in other literature.

The category of goals most often mentioned concern the adaptation of products, sites and services to the user's or buyer's personality, e.g. the background colour of a smartphone screen, the design of a website and, of course, all kinds of commercial and electoral promotion and messages to be shipped. The latter is also called micro-targeting being based on the presumption that socio-demographic attributes are but a proxy for attitutes and an individual's personal situation. By means of psychography, the personality of the people is to be addressed, not, like in the past, their presumed opinions, and this is to happen by means of facts about the respective person itself, not about groups of persons which they belong to and whose aggregated properties apply to them more or less accurately, only, but not necessarily exactly. This should increase the effectivity of advertising and marketing and foster the adaptation to the traditional mass media's loss of importance, the more fragmented media market and more segmented audiences (Agan 2007), by sending out emails and mail (so-called direct marketing) and on the doorstep (in case of political election campaigns). Interfaces like social media websites and e-commerce websites can already be adapted to the personality of single users (preferences for interaction styles in the digital world, Quercia et al. 2011: 1, web site morphing, ibid., p.6; „Knowing the users' personality can be a strategic advantage for the design of adaptive and personalized user interfaces." Oliveira et al. 2011: 2191), according to the similarity attraction law which psychological law says that similarity attracts (Reeves et al. 1996: 90, Vinciarelli 2014). Also, the advertisements which are shown to a user on a website can be adapted to his personality, and those product reviews whose authors are similar to him in regard to their personality can be put on the top of a list of search results. Recommendation services also belong to those free services which can be oriented to the user's personality, not only to relations independent from the it, e.g. the Twitter friendship recommendations. (Golbeck et al. 2011, p.6) A famous recommender system is that of amazon: "Customers who bought this item also bought ...". In the future, it could read "Customers who bought this item and have a personality structure similar to yours also bought ..."

It has been suggested to adapt a smartphone app which should animate the user to steady physical behaviour (sports) and present him for this purpose a list of games which suit his personality and motivate him by spoken sentences (adaption of spoken sentences to the user's personality). (Oliveira et al. 2011: 2193).

People need not to fill in long questionnaires, any more, to let assess their personality or have it analysed. This yields new possibilities for psychological research (Kosinski et al. 2013: 4), e.g. being able to collect informations about people's personality without administering a questionnaire to them (Youyou et al. 2015: 4), also on the national level – psychological classification of whole populations -, i.e. also for social scientific research (Monjoye et al. 2013). Furthermore, it facilitates remote diagnostics of mental illnesses and diseases for the purpose of medicinal treatment. (Kosinski et al. 2013: 4)

Another goal is the adaption of the behaviour of virtual agents and robots (e.g. household and service robots which scan permanently the disposition of their owners and respond to it socially) to the personality of their human interaction partners. Of course, regarding this aspect, it is also imaginable that more direct techniques are developed based on the agent's permanent recording of voice and video of the humans it is dealing with which are permanently analysed to track their personality as well as mood (properties of voice and speech which indicate stress or serenity, spoken utterances (also soliloquy), facial impression, movements) like the terminator from the equally named movie whose visual field resembles that of augmented reality glasses which analyse all things coming into their sight and put comments on it (for human beings: Google Glass etc.). Robots are even called potential romantic partners since they can understand their human partners better than fellow humans because of their analytical abilities (Youyou et al. 2015: 4). Here, the law of similarity attraction comes into play, again, in that artificial agents take on a personality similar to that of their human partners. Human beings can observe this virtually high sensibility of robots presumably to a particularly high degree if the latter deal with a multitude of individuals at the same time and adapt alternatingly to the personality of each of them. It should reinforce the perception of robots belonging to a new ontological category (standing between humans and machines, possessing some human traits) (Kahn et al. 2011, Kahn et al. 2012).

Other goals mentioned are:
- Detection of possible school schooters in the USA, and of people possessing pathological personalities presumably leading to assaults (Neuman 2016: 45ff.). Nota bene without considering opinions and beliefs, but only on the basis of psychological personality traits.
- Enterprises can improve their selection of new employees.
- In the future, people could rely more on automatic personality analysis than on their own or fellow human beings' judgements when choosing their acitivities, occupation and even their romantic partners (Youyou et al. 2015: 4).
- The realization of individuals Cyber-I could be facilitated, i.e. of a complete digital or data double of them (Lyon 2015: 83) being actively produced by themselves which would also require a correct copy of their personalities (Wen et al. 2009, Guo 2016).

Risks of automatic personality analysis mentioned are:
- People can be more easily manipulated and influenced if their personality traits are known (Youyou et al. 2015: 4). I think that in particular the influence on human preferences by non-argumentative factors and the context of arguments would be facilitated, i.e. by the formulation of arguments and their general presentation (kind and design of the medium of the message). If you know what someone finds pleasant or not and which weak points he has you can take this into account when addressing him in order to influence his acceptance of your address positively, by way of his emotions, not his intellect.
- Enterprises as well as governments could gain intimate knowledge about many people without their consent to or even notice of their data being collected and analysed to produce this kind of knowledge about them (Kosinski et al. 2013: 4).
- Wrong conclusions could be drawn about people (like in case of testing their creditworthiness, intellectual capability, health prospect) (Kosinski et al. 2013: 4). This can't be ruled out because of the stochastic character of the methodes applied (stochastic variation).
- Occurence of social sorting, i.e. individuals are categorized and as a result of this descriminated. They don't get particular chances any more, e.g. buying offers, credit offers, job offers, and what if it are some day rights which they aren't awarded any more or governmental action which is either exerted on them or precisely not. (Lyon 2015: 25f.)
- Violation of personal rights and personal privacy, even by analysis of seemingly non-revealing data and metadata produced by usage of e.g. social media and mobile telephony (Quercia et al. 2011).

To conclude, the field of automated personality analysis from online and mobile usage (big) data via computer program is a young field of research and development, several approaches exist and at least one mature technique (using Facebook-Likes). The methods of all of these approaches are generated following the same procedure: using data of persons whose personality traits are known (from a questionnaire), a large share of them for development of the method (formula, algorithm) and the remaining share to validate it afterwards. Claims of the US enterprise Cambridge Analytica made after the last US electoral campaign about the successful role of its psychographic voter analysis for addressing voters had to be abandoned.

But psychographic attributes are promoted by address trading enterprises to be included in the material they offer (Christl 2014: 54, 56), their nature and origin being not easily identifiable, though. Because of the good accessibility of Big Data about the population in the USA – privacy protection being much lower there than in Germany -, it's not probable that attempts to use them to analyse the personality of their originators will decline. In addition, automatic opinion mining and sentiment analysis of online product reviews and texts from online forums exist some years longer, already. To be able to apply all these methods to user data, it has to be legal. E.g. regarding the assessment of creditworthiness in Germany, there are legal prescriptions saying that every person who wants to initiate a commercial contract has to accept that a probability assessment of his future payment behaviour is carried out (Christl 2014: 55). If the aims of automatic personality analysis remain economic and related to commercial and electoral promotion no incisive effect on people's lifes should be expected. Only if they are misused by political or economic actors to peg people there will be the danger to discriminate against them in regard to informations given and offers made, freedom of choice and eventually even citizen rights. The philospher Plato has conceived a society in which philosopher kings recognize which occupation and activity can be carried out best by someone and have, at the same time, the power to compel him to take this occupation or activity – since it's "the best" for society. Even if it's not probable that such kind of assessment is done in the future by usage of Big Data from people collected by certain enterprises, it should be paid attention to if a tendency toward it isn't created by the collusion of public agencies and data collecting private enterprises. Not to speak of an explicit abuse of data and methods by dictatorial regimes to preserve their power.

How to evaluate automatic personality analysis sociologically under the condition of its mass application which doesn't yet exist?

Perhaps, an effect of it will be the emergence of a "personality bubble" around every online user leading him to feel himself better in the virtual world in which all agents are catering to him than in the real world in which he meets people he doesn't harmonize with. This notion is cast in analogy to that of filter bubble which means that individuals get personalized informations from search engines and other virtual agents, only, and, thus, miss to recognize the really existing diversity of facts and figures (blinker effect). Perhaps, above this, also products and services will increasingly be customized to the user's personality. Precondition for both is that the computer programs of virtual agents and the producers of the products and services have access to the results of the personality analysis. While the notion of filter bubble relates to content chosen by virtual agents and that of echo chamber to the receipt of news exclusively from websites which advance the same opinions and views as the user (Flaxman et al. 2016) the notion of personality bubble relates to the user's psychological personality to which all that comes across him online has been adjusted.

Weingart (1989: 189) denotes the effect of new technologies, of their perception, as "making hitherto existing expectations and behaviours contingent and opening up new horizons of expectations" (translation by S.S.). In the same vain, Anthony Giddens' argument that people today were constantly aware of the possibility that every aspect of their world could be revealed by science to be different from how it was currently conceived to be could be formulated as modern science making horizons of certainty contingent once and for all (not only in a punctual manner as Weingart sees it which isn't fully correct). From „The consequences of modernity" (Giddens 1992: 40): "No knowledge under conditions of modernity is knowledge in the "old" sense, where "to know" is to be certain. This applies equally to the natural and the social sciences." (p.39, lower part, is pertinent, too) So, the cool thing is that modern science doesn't create an awareness of the possession of a knowledge beyond faith and superstition and being finally correct, now, but, on the contrary, an awareness of that every part of reality is permanently put to test regarding its true nature and knowledge about it, thus, can always change making current knowledge obsolete (tentativeness of modern scientific knowledge).

Regarding personality analysis from digital data, uncertainty of knowledge is revealed, on the one hand, by the circumstance that something which had hitherto been largely unanalysed and unknown and been analysable only with a quite high amount of effort (administering a questionnaire) – individuals' personality - can now be analysed easily without people's collaboration and, providing the amount of case data necessary exist, with a very high throughput. Secondly, uncertainty of knowledge is revealed by the existence of the possibility that the assessment of an individual's personality yields a result different from his own self-perception and, thirdly, yields different results from different algorithms and from the use of different data. Fourthly, it is revealed by the existence of the possibility that in the future another personality model or another variation of the Big Five model turns out to be more appropriate and, thus, individuals' classification changes. In the latter two cases, individuals had to revise their picture of their own personality or to deal with differences between this picture and the result of automatic analyses of their personality anew. This is true also for third parties which conduct automatic personality analysis for commercial or political purposes. After a change of the data or the personality model used, they have eventually to admit the obsoleteness of their analysis based actions carried out so far and, in particular after the personality model has changed, to develop new strategies for addressing the now new existing personality types or traits.

Concerning the validity of the Big Five model, it has to be granted that it is also externally validated to a high degree, by its relations to other attitudes and behavious like job satisfaction, occupational position and achievement, choice of spouse and friends and political and consumer preferences (Golbeck et al. 2011b).

Therefore, it looks like that the personality model currently used will remain the same in the foreseeable future, at least.

Literature

Agan, Tom, Silent Marketing: Micro-targeting, A Penn, Schoen and Berland Associates White Paper, 2007

Anonymous, What Type of Web Data Can You Collect From Facebook, on: BrightPlanet.com, 17.06.2016, https://brightplanet.com/2016/06/type-web-data-can-collect-facebook/

Beuth, Patrick, Die Luftpumpen von Cambridge Analytica, in: ZEIT ONLINE, 07.03.2017

Chittaranjan, Gokul, Jan Blom, Daniel Gatica-Perez, Who's Who with Big-Five: Analyzing and Classifying Personality Traits with Smartphones, in: ISWC '11 Proceedings of the 2011 15th Annual International Symposium on Wearable Computers, p.29-36

Christl, Wolfie, Kommerzielle digitale Überwachung im Alltag, Studie im Auftrag der Bundesarbeitskammer, Wien, 2014

Confessore, Nicholas, Danny Hakim, Data Firm Says 'Secret Sauce' Aided Trump; Many Scoff, in: The New York Times, 06.03.2017

Dodge, Martin, Robin Kitchin, 'Outlines of a World Coming Into Existence': Pervasive Computing and the Ethics of Forgetting, in: Environment and Planning B: Planning and Design 2007, Vol.34, p.431-445

Dourish, Paul, Algorithms and Their Others: Algorithmic Culture in Context, in: Big Data & Society, 2016, Vol.3, No.2, p.1–11

Ferwerda, Bruce, Markus Schedl, Marko Tkalcic, Using Instagram Picture Features to Predict Users' Personality, in: Q. Tian et al. (Eds.): MMM 2016, Part I, Springer International Publishing Switzerland 2016, p.850–861

Flaxman, Seth, Sharad Goel, Justin M. Rao, Filter Bubbles, Echo Chambers, and Online News Consumption, in: Public Opinion Quarterly, Vol.80, Special Issue, 2016, p.298-320

Giddens, Anthony, The Consequences of Modernity, Cambridge: Polity Press, 1990

Golbeck, Jennifer, Predicting Personality from Social Media Text, in: Transactions on Replication Research, 2016, Vol.2, p.1-10

Golbeck, Jennifer, Cristina Robles, Michon Edmondson, Karen Turner, Predicting Personality from Twitter, in: 2011 IEEE International Conference on Privacy, Security, Risk, and Trust, and IEEE International Conference on Social Computing, 2011a, p.149-156

Golbeck, Jennifer, Cristina Robles, Karen Turner, Predicting Personality with Social Media, in: CHI '11 Extended Abstracts on Human Factors in Computing Systems, 2011b, p.253-262

Gou, Liang, Michelle X. Zhou, Huahai Yang, KnowMe and ShareMe: Understanding Automatically Discovered Personality Traits from Social Media and User Sharing Preferences, in: CHI '14 Proceedings of the SIGCHI Conference on Human Factors in Computing Systems, 2014, p.955-964

Grassegger, Hannes, Mikael Krogerus, Ich habe nur gezeigt, dass es die Bombe gibt, in: Das Magazin N°48, 3. Dezember 2016, www.dasmagazin.ch

Guo, Ao, A Smartphone-based System for Personal Data Management and Personality Analysis, 2016, download from http://repo.lib.hosei.ac.jp/bitstream/10114/12207/1/13t2007.pdf

Hartlmaier, Benjamin, Roman Leipold, Die geheime Macht der Daten, in: Chip 04/2017, p.34-38

Kahn Jr., Peter H., Takayuki Kanda, Hiroshi Ishiguro, Brian T. Gill, Jolina H. Ruckert, Solace Shen, Heather E. Gary, Aimee L. Reichert, Nathan G. Freier, Rachel L. Severson, Do People Hold a Humanoid Robot Morally Accountable for the Harm It Causes?, in: 2012 7th ACM/IEEE International Conference on Human-Robot Interaction (HRI 2012), 2012, p.33-40

Kahn Jr., Peter H., Aimee L. Reichert, Heather E. Gary, Takayuki Kanda, Hiroshi Ishiguro, Solace Shen, Jolina H. Ruckert, Brian Gill, The New Ontological Category Hypothesis in HumanRobot Interaction, in: 2011 6th ACM/IEEE International Conference on Human-Robot Interaction (HRI 2011), 2011, p.159-160

Kosinski, Michal, David Stillwell, Thore Graepel, Private Traits and Attributes Are Predictable from Digital Records of Human Behavior, in: Proceedings of the National Academy of Sciences of the United States of America, 2013, Vol.110, No.15, p.5802-5805

Lapowsky, Issie, A Lot of People Are Saying Trump's New Data Team Is Shady, in: Wired, 15.08.2016, www.wired.com

Liu, Bing, Lei Zhang, A Survey of Opinion Mining and Sentiment Analysis, in: Charu C. Aggarwal, ChengXiang Zhai, Mining Text Data, Springer: Boston, MA, 2013, p.415-463

Lyon, David, Surveillance after Snowden, Cambridge: Polity Press, 2015

Montjoye, Yves-Alexandre de, Jordi Quoidbach, Florent Robic, and Alex (Sandy) Pentland, Predicting Personality Using Novel Mobile Phone-Based Metrics, in: 2013 International Conference on Social Computing, Behavioral-Cultural Modeling, & Prediction (SBP13), Berlin, Heidelberg: Springer, 2013, p.48-55

Neuman, Yair, Computational Personality Analysis. Introduction, Practical Applications and Novel Directions, Cham: Springer, 2016

Oliveira, Rodrigo de, Alexandros Karatzoglou, Pedro Concejero, Ana Armenta, Nuria Oliver, Towards a Psychographic User Model From Mobile Phone Usage, in: CHI '11 Extended Abstracts on Human Factors in Computing Systems, 2011, p.2191-2196

Quercia, Daniele, Michal Kosinski, David Stillwell, Jon Crowcroft, Our Twitter Profiles, Our Selves: Predicting Personality with Twitter, in: 2011 IEEE Third International Conference on Privacy, Security, Risk and Trust and 2011 IEEE Third International Conference on Social Computing, p.180-185

Reeves, Byron, Clifford Nass, The Media Equation. How People Treat Computers, Television, and New Media Like Real People and Places, Cambridge: University Press, 1996

Richards, Neil M., Jonathan H. King, Three Paradoxes of Big Data, in: The Stanford Law Review Online, September 2013

Schwartz, H. Andrew, Johannes C. Eichstaedt, Margaret L. Kern, Lukasz Dziurzynski, Stephanie M. Ramones, Megha Agrawal, Achal Shah, Michal Kosinski, David Stillwell, Martin E. P. Seligman, Lyle H. Ungar, Personality, Gender, and Age in the Language of Social Media: The Open-Vocabulary Approach, in: PLOS ONE, 2013, Vol.8, No.9, www.plosone.org

Takahashi, Dean, IBM Researcher Can Decipher Your Personality from Looking at 200 of Your Tweets, 08.10.2013, heruntergeladen von https://venturebeat.com/2013/10/08/ibm-researcher-can-decipher-your-personality-in-200-tweets/

Vinciarelli, Alessandro, A Survey of Personality Computing, IEEE Transactions on Affective Computing, 2014, Vol.5, No.3, p.273-291

Weingart, Peter, "Großtechnische Systeme" – Ein Paradigma der Verknüpfung von Technikentwicklung und sozialem Wandel?, in: ibid. (Ed.), Technik als sozialer Prozeß, Frankfurt am Main: Suhrkamp, 1989, S.174-196

Wen, Jie, Kai Ming, Furong Wang, Benxiong Huang, Jianhua Ma, Cyber-I: Vision of the Individual's Counterpart on Cyberspace, in: 2009 Eighth IEEE International Conference on Dependable, Autonomic and Secure Computing, p.295-302

Yang, Huahai, Yunyao Li, Identifying User Needs from Social Media, IBM Research Report RJ10513 (ALM1309-013) September 23, 2013

Youyou, Wu, Michael Kosinski, David Stillwell, Computer-based Personality Judgments Are More Accurate than Those Made by Humans, in: Proceedings of the National Academy of Sciences of the United States of America, 2015, Vol.112, No.4, p.1036-1040

Zhou, Michelle X., Jeffrey Nichols, Thomas Dignan, Jennifer Golbeck, Steve Lohr, Jeffrey Hancock, Opportunities and Risks of Discovering Personality Traits from Social Media, in: CHI '14 Extended Abstracts on Human Factors in Computing Systems, 2014, p.1081-1086

YOUR KNOWLEDGE HAS VALUE

- We will publish your bachelor's and master's thesis, essays and papers

- Your own eBook and book - sold worldwide in all relevant shops

- Earn money with each sale

Upload your text at www.GRIN.com and publish for free